ice cream
mix-ins

ice cream mix-ins

EASY HOMEMADE TREATS

jeff keys

Photography by Zac Williams

GIBBS SMITH
TO ENRICH AND INSPIRE HUMANKIND

Salt Lake City | Charleston | Santa Fe | Santa Barbara

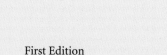

First Edition
13 12 11 10 09   5 4 3 2 1

Published by
Gibbs Smith
P.O. Box 667
Layton, Utah 84041

Orders: 1.800.835.4993
www.gibbs-smith.com

Designed by Dawn DeVries Sokol
Printed and bound in China

Gibbs Smith books are printed on either recycled, 100% post consumer waste, or FSC certified papers.

Library of Congress Cataloging-in-Publication Data

Keys, Jeff.
  Ice cream mix-ins : easy homemade treats / Jeff Keys ; photographs by Zac
Williams. — 1st ed.
     p. cm.
  ISBN-13: 978-1-4236-0453-2
  ISBN-10: 1-4236-0453-9
  1. Ice cream, ices, etc. I. Title.
  TX795.K488 2009
  641.8'62—dc22
                    2008035670

contents

To

my grandparents

Clint and Marion Dyer

acknowledgments

I'd like to thank Gibbs Smith for the opportunity to create this book. It is always a privilege and a blessing.

To my editor, Jennifer Grillone, you are always there and I thank you for that.

To Zac Williams, thanks for an amazing and intense photo shoot. What a great job! You definitely know what you are doing and were fun and easy to work with.

To my wife, Sheila, and the boys, thanks for putting up with me while I was creating the book and running a busy restaurant. It is always great to come home.

And to my restaurant family, I know it is not easy but you always come through.

introduction

I am standing at the foot of two gravestones in the sprawling cemetery of a windy town in northeast Texas. My nineteen-year-old son, Austin, stands with me and it is spring in Texas and wildflowers are blooming on the roadsides and a south wind is blowing up in our faces. We have come to Royce City, Texas, on a mission of discovery and we have found our first clue: the final resting place of Estelle and RZ Dyer, victims of the influenza epidemic that stormed through Texas in the winter of 1912–13. Estelle and RZ were the parents of young Clinton C. Dyer, who was fourteen years old at the time they died. Clint, later in life, exactly forty-two years later, would become my grandfather, but on this day in the spring of 2008 my son and I stand in silence over the gravestones and marvel that we have uncovered a lost link that I have wondered about for half of my life. Here we are in the land of my grandfather, where he found himself on his own at the age of fourteen. The question that must have gone through his mind was "How will I survive?" I feel like life is a mystery, and here we are, my son and I, about to see a long lost mystery unfold. "And what," you may ask, "does this have to do with an ice cream book?" Be patient with me, for here is that story.

In 1912, Royce City was a small town thirty-one miles east of Dallas on the old rail line falling away to the lowlands of Louisiana. It was cotton country, and Royce City was a prosperous town. It had three cotton gin mills to process the cotton that thrived in the humid farmlands that swayed away from town in all directions like the bent spokes of a bicycle wheel. There were restaurants and hotels and the rail line from Dallas that brought city people out to the countryside for nights of dining and fun, a short vacation from normal routine. Downtown Royce City was very attractive and typically Texas with its quaint red brick buildings lining Main Street. On the corner of Main Street and Arch there stood Royce City Drug, with its soda fountain and ice cream parlor. An old-fashioned ice cream parlor. How we wish some of those were still around. But, of course, it wasn't old-fashioned then. It was what was happening in a busy little beehive of a town. Very modern in fact. And thank goodness it was there, for it became the home of my grandfather Clint. It became his refuge and center of gravity. When Clint's parents both passed in the influenza epidemic, he was left on his own to fend for himself. He was too old for the social services of the time, and lacking other family, he was swept into life on his own. Years later and many worlds away when I came tumbling out of the mists, he would tell me the stories of his life as an orphaned boy in Texas and how he found his way in the world.

My grandfather was a natural storyteller and a great lover of words. Any time we were together the stories would come flowing out. They were great stories and fun to listen to. Stories about literally living on ice cream after has parents passed away and learning the ice cream trade at Royce City Drug. Stories of playing high school football and being thrown off the team for playing too rough. Imagine that, in Texas! A kid alone might have a few things to work out.

My grandfather was not a large man when you measure by height, but he had a presence and was compact and strong. When he shook hands, you felt the grip of a confident working man who had no apologizes. He was not shy about expressing an opinion or starting a project that required a lot of work. He had an inner strength that scared me sometimes, but I was drawn to it also. He figured things out if he wanted to accomplish something or if his back was up against a wall. Throughout his life he was always building something, designing something, or coming up with some newfangled idea to get things done.

So one evening in the 1950s when my family went to my grandparents' house for dinner, he called me out to the back porch. There on the porch sat a large round wooden tub filled with ice and salt and melted ice water. Inside that tub was a smaller steel tub with a handle coming out the top, and Pop (that's what I called my grandfather) was churning away. You could smell the salt water and the wood and the steel, and it made my mouth taste salty and metallic. It was a fine chemistry. He was making homemade ice cream, the first I would ever eat. When dinner was over, the level of excitement was thick in the air. My sisters and I couldn't wait to see what was in that steel tub. We knew it was ice cream, but it was still a mystery. I'll never forget the moment when Pop removed the lid from that tub, for inside was the prettiest, creamiest, most sparkling and delicious smelling vanilla ice cream I had ever seen. It was the ice cream that my grandfather had learned to make in Texas in 1912.

My grandfather passed away in early January of 1974 after a short battle with pancreatic cancer. In the fall of 1973 he had helped me dig a new water well at a little farm I had in Ashland, Oregon. Pop was seventy-seven years old then and he was still stronger than I was. He worked hard to the end of each day and never failed to push me to new levels that I didn't know I had. Every evening after finishing up a long day of work, he would have his shot of 10 High bourbon whiskey under the awning of his travel trailer and then we would have dinner. But he just wasn't right, and I could feel it. My grandmother said his stomach was hurting, but he never said anything about it.

After my grandparents left the farm, with winter coming on, and returned to Southern California, I would get word from my mom, occasionally, that Pop was hurting and going in for tests. Christmas came and I was busy being the head chef of an Ashland restaurant six days a week and going through the usual chaotic Christmas and New Year's rush. One afternoon I got a call from Pop and he wondered where I was.

I'll never forget that call. He was very disoriented and I heard something I had never heard before from my grandfather, the sound of fear in his voice. I told him that I would come down to see him as soon as the holiday rush was over. Pop was in the hospital with a bad diagnosis, and I don't believe that anyone in the family realized how sick he really was. Needless to say, it was very hard to keep chefing and not leave immediately for Southern California. But I had a job to finish and so I stayed. We closed the restaurant to take a week off the day after New Year's and drove straight through to the southland in a blinding snowstorm in fifteen hours. When we got to my parents' home late that night my mom opened the door and burst into tears. Pop had passed away earlier that day.

Two years later I was in Crested Butte, Colorado, working on my own restaurant, partnered with my best friend from my college years, Nick Lypps. We were working long days but having a lot of fun because the restaurant was becoming a success. One night after work I was in bed, writing something and dozing off to sleep when I heard the distinct sound of my grandfather's voice call out my name. "Jeff," he said. I sat straight up in bed and in perfect innocence responded, "Pop?" but I heard nothing else. I was not afraid, and I felt a rush of emotion hearing the clarity of my grandfather's voice. That was the last time I heard from Pop, but he left me with a legacy from his stories and his strength.

Crested Butte led me to other restaurants in other places. I was always a bit of a vagabond. But finally I arrived in Sun Valley, Idaho, with my wife, Sheila, and we have built a life in the food world here. And ice cream is a major part of that life. We call our ice creams Mountain Decadence Ice Cream, and one cannot think of our restaurant without thinking about Mountain Decadence. It's my term for our ice cream as well as for the good life in the mountains. The term has a special meaning for our clientele and after all these years I still get a kick out of creating new flavors and dessert creations from our ice cream. That is just my grandfather coming out in me. So here for you is the taste of Mountain Decadence Ice Cream. I truly hope you enjoy the ice cream and the line of history as it stretches all the way back to that little town in windy east Texas in 1912, where a soda fountain and ice cream parlor literally rescued a young man's life and started him on a path that resonates today almost one hundred years later. Enjoy the book!

a brief note on ice cream

I think that ice cream is architecture. It is a structure and you design it. I'm not going to get all scientific on you. For me that would take the magic out of the creation. But I do want to give you a way to think about it so you have a vision of what you are doing.

Again, ice cream is a structure. It is a structure of ice crystals blended with air, and the smaller the ice crystals the smoother the ice cream. You get small ice crystals from a really cold and fast freezing process. It's just like in the middle of winter when it's really cold, you get really light snow because the ice crystals are so tiny. In the spring when it warms up and it snows, the snowflakes are huge and heavy. Well, it's like that with ice cream. Smaller crystals, smoother ice cream.

The best advice I can give you, then, to make great ice cream at home is to find an ice cream maker that gets really cold and makes the ice cream fast. There are a lot of ice cream makers on the market to choose from, and my favorites are usually made in Italy. Those sleek Italian ice cream makers that look like a little Ferrari, the great Italian racecar. They come in countertop models, all shiny stainless steel and the peak of design. I have one in the kitchen of my restaurant,

and I never miss the chance to show it to someone. It's the closest I'll ever get to owning a real Ferrari. But really, there are lots of ice cream makers that work just great. There's the churn freezer that uses ice and rock salt that works great. That's what my grandfather was using way back when, but they come with electric motors now.

I've geared my ice cream recipes to make about 1½ quarts of ice cream so that most home ice cream makers will work with these recipes as far as capacity goes. If you find that you have too much mix for a single batch, simply make the ice cream in two batches.

mix-ins

On a special note, with all of the ice cream recipes in this book, feel free to make your own variations or additions by mixing in your favorite things. These recipes are guides, and none of them are ever in their final form. You might discover after a couple of tries that you would like more or less of one ingredient or another. The vanilla ice creams especially lend themselves well to adding additional goodies when they come out of the ice cream machine and the ice cream is still relatively soft. Try mixing in your favorite cookies, chopped up of course. Or try mixing in toasted nuts, or chocolate chips, or a few spoonfuls of your favorite jam. I love to swirl in one of our dessert sauces that you'll find later in the book. The possibilities are endless and that makes it more enjoyable and a lot of fun. So free yourself and be a little crazy. What sounds good to you?

vanilla
ice creams

i'm sitting at a dining table in my restaurant, Vintage, in Ketchum, Idaho. It is late afternoon. I'm beginning a short introduction to my vanilla ice creams that will appear in this book. There is a plate of warm vanilla beans from Veracruz, Mexico, sitting in front of me on the table for inspiration. The aroma of the vanilla is wafting up and filling the room, and I'm taking it in. I'm beginning to relax, and the stress of a day in the food world is slipping away. And that, in a nutshell, is what the Totonaca people along the gulf coast of what is now Mexico experienced seven hundred years ago when they discovered the vanilla bean, the only edible fruit in the orchid family.

The history is fascinating. The Totonaca teaching it to the Maya. The Azteca conquering the Maya and taking vanilla and chocolate back to Montezuma. Cortes conquering the Azteca and sending the first vanilla back to Europe. Thomas Jefferson, after completing his ambassadorship to France in 1789 and having experienced vanilla in Paris, finding no word of vanilla back in the United States and ordering fifty vanilla pods shipped from France to the U.S. The history is compelling and many layered, and nobody tells it better than Patricia Rain, the Vanilla Queen. You can go to www.vanilla.com for all the history on the amazing vanilla bean. The site is also a tremendous resource of the very best vanilla beans and extracts and anything else having to do with vanilla. (I have no personal connection to this company other than I think it is the best source available.) Now, on to the ice creams.

∘ philadelphia vanilla bean ∘

This recipe is one of the earliest recorded ice cream recipes from the United States. It is still great today after all of these years. It is simple, pure, and easy to make, and it's a great place to start an ice cream adventure.

2 cups whipping cream
2 cups whole milk
6 vanilla beans
1 cup sugar
½ cup light corn syrup

Pour the cream and milk into a medium-size stainless steel bowl and place over a steaming pan of boiling water. When the mix gets hot, a film will form over the surface.

While the mix is scalding, cut the vanilla beans in half lengthwise and scrape out the seeds with a spoon. Add the vanilla bean pods and seeds and the sugar to the cream mix; let steep over the steaming water for about 5 minutes. Remove bowl from heat and let the mix cool to room temperature, and then chill completely in the refrigerator. You can make the ice cream now, or for a fuller and more developed flavor, cover and let the mix rest overnight in the refrigerator.

Before making the ice cream, remove the bean pods with a slotted spoon and discard, and then add the corn syrup. Pour the mix into an ice cream maker and process according to the manufacturer's instructions. Scoop the finished ice cream into a container and then place in the freezer to cure and harden. This ice cream brings out the essence of vanilla and it tastes great. *Makes 8 servings.*

∘ rich vanilla ∘

Rich Vanilla ice cream is a creamier and more lush version of the Philadelphia Vanilla Bean ice cream. It is made from a vanilla custard mixture that is similar to Philadelphia Vanilla Bean but with the addition of egg yolks and a little instant coffee. With this ice cream, you can substitute pure vanilla extract for the vanilla beans and it will work out fine.

2 cups whipping cream

2 cups whole milk

6 vanilla beans or 2 tablespoons pure vanilla extract

1 cup sugar

¾ teaspoon instant coffee crystals

8 fresh egg yolks

½ cup light corn syrup

Pour the cream and milk into a medium-size stainless steel bowl and place over a steaming pan of boiling water. When the mix gets hot, a film will form over the surface.

While the mix is scalding, cut the vanilla beans in half lengthwise, if using, and scrape out the seeds with a spoon. Add the vanilla bean pods and seeds or the pure vanilla extract. Add the sugar and instant coffee; let steep for about 5 minutes.

With a wire whip, stir in the egg yolks, whisking until thoroughly blended. Cook the mix over the steaming pot for about 10 more minutes. Stir with the whip occasionally so it cooks evenly. Remove from the heat and let the mix cool to room temperature, and then chill completely in the refrigerator. You can make the ice cream now, or for a fuller and more developed flavor, cover and let the mix rest overnight in the refrigerator.

Before making the ice cream, remove the bean pods, if used, with a slotted spoon, and then add the corn syrup. Pour the mix into an ice cream maker and process according to the manufacturer's instructions. Scoop the ice cream into a container and then place in the freezer to cure and harden. *Makes 8 servings.*

• malted cookies and cream •

This may be my very favorite mix-in recipe, as Oreo cookies and malted milk powder add so much flavor to the vanilla ice cream. I hope you enjoy this is much as I do and begin to feel free to create your own mix-in ice cream ideas as well!

homemade version

*1 recipe Rich Vanilla ice cream
  (page 16)
16 Oreo cookies, coarsely chopped
4 tablespoons Carnation Malted
  Milk Powder*

Make the Rich Vanilla ice cream according to the recipe. When the ice cream is ready, scoop it into a chilled bowl and quickly and gently fold in the Oreo cookies and malted milk powder. If you are a fan of malts at your ice cream shop, you'll love this ice cream. If you're not such a fan of malt, leave out the malted milk powder and you'll still have a great cookies and cream ice cream. Put the ice cream in a container and then place in the freezer to cure and harden. *Makes 8 servings.*

easy mix-in version

Replace the Rich Vanilla ice cream with 1 quart premium store-bought vanilla ice cream. Soften the ice cream and follow the rest of the instructions above.

° orange blossom honey vanilla °

The orange blossom honey in this recipe adds an exotic quality to the ice cream. It's my favorite honey. It reminds me of when I was a kid and had my first honey ice cream at our local ice cream shop. There was something magic about it that I've never forgotten.

2 cups whipping cream
2 cups whole milk
5 vanilla beans or 2 tablespoons
   pure vanilla extract
1 cup orange blossom honey
8 fresh egg yolks

Pour the cream and milk into a medium-size stainless steel bowl and place over a steaming pan of boiling water. When the mix gets hot, a film will form over the surface.

While the mix is scalding, cut the vanilla beans in half lengthwise, if using, and scrape out the seeds with a spoon. Add the vanilla bean pods and seeds or the pure vanilla extract to the mix. Add the honey.

With a wire whip, blend in the egg yolks, stirring constantly until well blended; let steep over the steaming water for about 10 minutes while stirring occasionally. Remove from the heat and let the mix cool to room temperature, then chill completely in the refrigerator.

Before making the ice cream, remove the bean pods, if used, with a slotted spoon. Pour the mix into an ice cream maker and process according to the manufacturer's instructions. Scoop the ice cream into a container and then place in the freezer to cure and harden. *Makes 8 servings.*

vanilla ice creams

◦ sicilian vanilla ◦

This is the first homemade ice cream I made. It was in Crested Butte, Colorado, in 1976 at my first restaurant, Soupcon. I decided I'd follow my grandfather's inspiration and make my own ice cream. I really don't remember that first recipe. I just know that I had some Sicilian crème de marsala, vanilla extract, and walnuts in the kitchen and took it from there. To my great surprise, the ice cream turned out to be delicious, and Sicilian Vanilla became a regular on our dessert roster. Here is how I make the ice cream today.

homemade version

2 cups whipping cream

2 cups whole milk

1 cup sugar

Pinch of fresh grated nutmeg

2 tablespoons pure vanilla extract

9 fresh egg yolks

2 tablespoons crème de marsala, preferably Sicilian

¾ cup chopped and toasted walnuts

Pour the cream and milk into a medium-size stainless steel bowl and place over a steaming pan of boiling water. When the mix gets hot, a film will form over the surface.

Add the sugar, nutmeg, and pure vanilla extract. With a wire whip, blend in the egg yolks, stirring constantly until well blended; let steep about 10 minutes. Add the crème de marsala. Remove from the heat and let the mix cool to room temperature, and then chill completely in the refrigerator.

Pour the mix into an ice cream maker and process according to the manufacturer's instructions. Add the walnuts to the ice cream when it is nearly done. Scoop the ice cream into a container and then place in the freezer to cure and harden. *Makes 8 servings.*

easy mix-in version

1 quart premium store-bought
  vanilla ice cream
Pinch of fresh grated nutmeg
2 tablespoons crème de marsala,
  preferably Sicilian
¾ cup chopped and toasted
  walnuts

Soften the ice cream and place in a medium-size mixing bowl. Fold in the nutmeg, crème de marsala, and walnuts. Return ice cream to container and then to freezer to cure and harden.

° veracruz vanilla °

In Veracruz, Mexico, they make a wonderful flan with vanilla beans and lime zest. I just had to adapt this simple combination to an ice cream. The ice cream turns out creamy from the custard mix, refreshing from the lime zest, and fragrant from the vanilla beans.

homemade version

2 cups whipping cream

2 cups whole milk

4 vanilla beans or 2 tablespoons
   pure Mexican vanilla extract

Zest of 2 limes

8 fresh egg yolks

Pour the cream and milk into a medium-size stainless steel bowl and place over a steaming pan of boiling water. When the mix gets hot, a film will form over the surface.

While the mix is scalding, cut the vanilla beans in half lengthwise, if using, and scrape out the seeds with a spoon. Add the vanilla bean pods and seeds or the pure Mexican vanilla extract and the zest to the mix.

With a wire whip, blend in the egg yolks, stirring constantly until well blended; let steep over the steaming water for about 10 minutes while stirring occasionally. Remove from the heat and let the mix cool to room temperature, and then chill completely in the refrigerator.

Before making the ice cream, remove the bean pods, if used, with a slotted spoon. Pour the mix into an ice cream maker and process according to the manufacturer's instructions. Scoop the ice cream into a container and then place in the freezer to cure and harden. This ice cream is a great way to experience two of Mexico's greatest flavors, vanilla and lime. *Makes 8 servings.*

easy mix-in version

1 quart premium store-bought
  vanilla ice cream

Zest of 2 limes

Soften the ice cream and place in a medium-size mixing bowl. Fold the lime zest into the softened ice cream. Return ice cream to container and put in freezer to cure and harden.

chocolate
ice creams

Chocolate has such a mystique. From the jungles of Mexico, it has spread around the entire world. We eat mountains of it. We give it to our friends, our kids, our lovers. Some cultures think a little bit of chocolate every day makes them healthier, happier, virile, relaxed, and full of vitality. Who could disagree with Montezuma, Elvis, or Emeril? I've almost always got my favorite chocolate bar stashed in a side pocket of my truck just in case I get that hunger. And what's my favorite? A Hershey's Symphony Bar with toffee and almonds. It reminds me of my dad.

Commercial chocolate ice cream has never quite made it with me. I've never found a great one. What I've discovered is it's the quality of the chocolate that counts. The recipes in this chapter are simple. They let the chocolate stand out. When it melts in your mouth something happens in the pleasure centers of your brain. In that way, you do become healthier, happier, virile, relaxed, and full of vitality. So here are some simple chocolate ice cream recipes, from the heart of Mountain Decadence Ice Cream country to you.

° rich chocolate °

This is my basic recipe for great chocolate ice cream. Many variations can be made from it, much like a jazz musician who takes a basic theme and then does riffs and spontaneous changes over a great song. So warm yourself up, because here we go.

2 cups whipping cream

2 cups whole milk

1 cup sugar

2 tablespoons pure vanilla extract

*2 tablespoons Dutch process cocoa
  powder*

Pinch of kosher salt

*12 ounces bittersweet or semisweet
  chocolate, cut into pieces*

7 fresh egg yolks

Pour the cream and milk into a medium-size stainless steel bowl and place over a steaming pan of boiling water. When the mix gets hot, a film will form over the surface.

Add the sugar, vanilla, cocoa powder, and salt. Blend thoroughly with a wire whip and then add the chocolate. Stir the mix gently while chocolate melts. When thoroughly blended, whisk in the egg yolks and continue stirring until the egg yolks are totally incorporated; let steep for about 6 or 7 minutes, stirring every few minutes so it cooks evenly. Remove from the heat and let the mix cool to room temperature, and then chill completely in the refrigerator.

Pour the mix into an ice cream maker and process according to the manufacturer's instructions. Scoop the ice cream into a container and then place in the freezer to cure and harden. Are you ready for some great chocolate ice cream? *Makes 8 servings.*

◦ chocolate kentucky bourbon ◦

When I think of Kentucky I think of Blue Grass, horses, the Kentucky Derby, and the best bourbon in the world. It gives such a kick to chocolate that, of course, I added some to chocolate ice cream. Here it is. Enjoy.

homemade version

1 recipe Rich Chocolate ice cream (page 24)

½ cup Kentucky bourbon

Following the directions for Rich Chocolate ice cream, add the bourbon 5 minutes after you've added the egg yolks; steep about 5 minutes more, stirring occasionally to blend and cook evenly. Follow the rest of the instructions and you have finished your first riff. *Makes 8 servings.*

easy mix-in version

Replace the Rich Chocolate ice cream with 1 quart premium store-bought chocolate ice cream. Soften the ice cream and place in a medium-size mixing bowl. Fold in ¼ to ½ cup Kentucky bourbon. Return ice cream to container and put in freezer to cure and harden.

° chocolate raspberry truffle °

This ice cream reminds me of France, where foods and treats are part of the national consciousness. The French expect exciting tastes every day. This is one of them!

homemade version

1 recipe Rich Chocolate ice cream
  (page 24)
10 ounces seedless red
  raspberry jam

Following the directions for Rich Chocolate ice cream, add the raspberry jam 5 minutes after you've added the egg yolks. Stir with a wire whip so the jam melts and is thoroughly incorporated; let steep about 5 minutes more. Follow the rest of the instructions to finish. Like any good jazz musician, you can go on all night doing these variations. Think of other liquors you like. Think of other jams that would complement or enhance chocolate. I think you get the idea! *Makes 8 servings.*

easy mix-in version

Replace the Rich Chocolate ice cream with 1 quart premium store-bought chocolate ice cream. Soften the ice cream and place in a medium-size mixing bowl. In the meantime, heat the jam in a small saucepan over medium heat or in the microwave. Stir the jam into the softened ice cream. Return ice cream to container and put in freezer to cure and harden.

chocolate ice creams

° burnt chocolate °

I call this ice cream Burnt Chocolate because we caramelize some of the sugar, which is slightly burning the sugar to a medium-dark amber colored syrup, before adding it to the cream mix. This in effect gives the ice cream a deeper, darker flavor. It intensifies the flavor of the chocolate. This is my most outlaw version of chocolate ice cream! Rich, dark, uncompromising, exotic—it's the red light district, the Marseilles of chocolate ice creams. It's even a bit dangerous to make, what with the caramelized sugar. So be careful, you might not look at chocolate ice cream the same way again.

2 cups whipping cream
2 cups whole milk
1½ cups sugar, divided
2 tablespoons pure vanilla extract
12 ounces bittersweet or semisweet
  chocolate, cut in pieces
Pinch of kosher salt
7 fresh egg yolks
3 tablespoons water

Pour the cream and milk into a medium-size stainless steel bowl and place over a steaming pan of boiling water. When the mix gets hot, a film will form over the surface. Add ½ cup sugar, vanilla extract, chocolate, and salt. Let the chocolate melt into the mix and stir with a wire whip until well blended. Stir in the egg yolks until they are thoroughly incorporated; let steep while you caramelize the rest of the sugar.

To caramelize the remaining sugar, put it in a small saucepan and add the water. Begin cooking the sugar mixture over medium-high heat. The sugar will dissolve and begin to bubble and caramelize. It will turn a nice amber color around the edges of the saucepan. Stir the sugar mixture with a wire whip and continue cooking until the syrup has become an even medium-dark amber color. Now it is ready to add to the ice cream mix. This is the dangerous part. The caramelized sugar is very hot. Use a pair of gloves to protect your hands and pour the sugar slowly into the ice cream mix. This will cause a little splattering, so do it slowly.

(continued on page 30)

Stir in the caramelized sugar until it is thoroughly blended into the mix. Remove from the heat and let the mix cool to room temperature, and then chill completely in the refrigerator.

Pour the mix into an ice cream maker and process according to the manufacturer's instructions. Scoop the ice cream into a container and then place in the freezer to cure and harden. Now a new ice cream experience awaits you! *Makes 8 servings.*

◦ chocolate grand marnier ◦

This ice cream is the essence of cool.

homemade version

*1 recipe Rich Chocolate ice cream
  (page 24)*
½ cup Grand Marnier

Following the directions for Rich Chocolate ice cream, add the Grand Marnier 5 minutes after you've added the egg yolks; steep about 5 minutes more, stirring occasionally to blend and cook evenly. Follow the rest of the instructions and you have finished another riff! When you take your first bite, think of a jazz club in Paris past midnight. *Makes 8 servings.*

easy mix-in version

Replace the Rich Chocolate ice cream with 1 quart premium store-bought chocolate ice cream. Soften the ice cream and place in a medium-size mixing bowl. Fold in the Grand Marnier. Return ice cream to container and put in freezer to cure and harden.

° creamy milk chocolate malt °

For any of you with fond remembrances of youth and time spent in your favorite soda fountain with young friends and lovers huddled over a delicious chocolate malt, this ice cream is for you. This ice cream is my homage to those times when you really didn't have a care in the world.

homemade version

2 cups whipping cream

2 cups whole milk

1 cup sugar

2 tablespoons pure vanilla extract

¾ cup Carnation Malted Milk

Pinch of kosher salt

*12 ounces milk chocolate, cut
  into pieces*

8 fresh egg yolks

Pour the cream and milk into a medium-size stainless steel bowl and place over a steaming pan of boiling water. When the mix gets hot, a film will form over the surface.

Add the sugar, vanilla, malted milk, and salt. Blend thoroughly with a wire whip and then add the chocolate. Stir the mix gently while chocolate melts. With a wire whip, stir in the egg yolks until they are thoroughly incorporated. Remove from the heat and let the mix cool to room temperature, and then chill completely in the refrigerator.

Pour the mix into an ice cream maker and process according to the manufacturer's instructions. Scoop the ice cream into a container and then place in the freezer to cure and harden. *Makes 8 servings.*

easy mix-in version

1 quart premium store-bought
  chocolate ice cream

¾ cup Carnation Malted Milk

12 ounces milk chocolate, cut
  into pieces

Soften the ice cream and place in a medium-size mixing bowl. Fold the malted milk and chocolate pieces into the softened ice cream. Return ice cream to container and put in freezer to cure and harden. You can also add chopped up cookies as a great mix-in to this recipe.

○ mexican chocolate ○

This is one of my favorite ice creams. It comes from the culture that gave us both vanilla and chocolate. Mexico has a long tradition of making its own unique style of chocolate. In Mexico, chocolate is made with a little cinnamon in it. Sometimes you also find it with finely ground almonds. In this ice cream I also use pure Mexican vanilla that comes from Veracruz, where the very best Mexican vanilla is made. I hope to capture some of the same magic that those mysterious and lost cultures, the Maya and the Azteca, discovered with chocolate and vanilla in the mystic jungles of the ancient past.

homemade version

2 cups whipping cream

2 cups whole milk

1 cup brown sugar

4 tablespoons pure Mexican vanilla, hopefully from Veracruz

12 to 14 ounces Mexican Chocolate (I prefer Ibarra Chocolate)

8 fresh egg yolks

½ cup toasted and chopped skinless slivered almonds

Pour the cream and milk into a medium-size stainless steel bowl and place over a steaming pan of boiling water. When the mix gets hot, a film will form over the surface.

Add the sugar and vanilla. Blend thoroughly with a wire whip and then add the chocolate. Stir the mix gently while the chocolate melts. When thoroughly blended, whisk in the egg yolks and continue stirring until the egg yolks are totally incorporated; let steep for about 6 or 7 minutes, stirring every few minutes so it cooks evenly. Remove from the heat and let the mix cool to room temperature, and then chill completely in the refrigerator.

Pour the mix into an ice cream maker and process according to the manufacturer's instructions. Add the almonds to the ice cream when nearly done. Scoop the ice cream into a container and then place in the freezer to cure and harden. *Makes 8 servings.*

easy mix-in version

1 quart premium store-bought
  chocolate ice cream
2 tablespoons pure Mexican vanilla,
  hopefully from Veracruz
½ cup toasted and chopped
  skinless slivered almonds

Soften the ice cream and place in a medium-size mixing bowl. Fold the vanilla, cinnamon, and almonds into the softened ice cream. Return ice cream to container and put in freezer to cure and harden.

° white chocolate °

White chocolate is a confection of sugar, cocoa butter, and milk solids. Officially, it cannot be called chocolate at all because it does not contain chocolate liquor or cocoa solids. But we call it white chocolate anyway. The French, the Swiss, and the Germans make great white chocolate, and it is delicious no matter what you call it. The deal with all chocolates, no matter what kind, is quality. And the best are usually from one of the countries I just mentioned. So when you make this ice cream, get a really good white chocolate.

2 cups whipping cream
2 cups whole milk
¾ cup sugar
2 tablespoons pure vanilla extract
Pinch of kosher salt
12 ounces white chocolate
7 egg yolks

Pour the cream and milk into a medium-size stainless steel bowl and place over a steaming pan of boiling water. When the mix gets hot, a film will form over the surface. Add the sugar, vanilla, and salt. Blend thoroughly with a wire whip and then add the white chocolate. Stir the mix gently while the chocolate melts.

When thoroughly blended, whisk in the egg yolks and continue stirring until the egg yolks are totally incorporated; let steep for about 6 or 7 minutes, stirring every few minutes so it cooks evenly. Remove from the heat and let the mix cool to room temperature, and then chill completely in the refrigerator.

Pour the mix into an ice cream maker and process according to the manufacturer's instructions. Scoop the ice cream into a container and then place in the freezer to cure and harden. *Makes 8 servings.*

coffee
ice creams

I love my cup of coffee. Every day. It's like a ritual I use around noon each day to let me know its time to get moving. I don't know if it's the coffee itself that gets me going or just the act that turns on the switch. That may be the only cup I have all day, but after that I am truly motivated. I like my coffee full-bodied, dark, rich, and smooth, and to me those are the qualities that I'm looking for in really good coffee ice cream. So that is what we are going to do. Make full-bodied, dark, rich, and smooth coffee ice cream. The first coffee ice cream we are going to make is called Shot of Coffee ice cream. It is the mother ice cream of our coffee family. Using the Shot of Coffee recipe as our base will enable us to make a nice variety of coffee-themed ice creams.

• shot of coffee •

This is my basic coffee ice cream. From this recipe you can make some nice variations that are simple and fun to accomplish and will give you just the right coffee ice cream for any special occasion.

2 cups whipping cream

2 cups whole milk

1 cup sugar

3 tablespoons pure vanilla extract

2 tablespoons plus 1 teaspoon instant espresso powder (I like Medaglia D'Oro)

½ cup whole Italian roast coffee beans

8 fresh egg yolks

½ cup light corn syrup

Pour the cream and milk into a medium-size stainless steel bowl and place over a steaming pan of boiling water. When the mix gets hot, a film will form over the surface.

Add the sugar, vanilla, espresso powder, and coffee beans to the mix; let cook for about 5 minutes, bringing all the flavors of the coffee together. Stir in the egg yolks with a wire whip to make sure all of the yolks are blended into the mix; let steep about 10 minutes more, stirring every few minutes so it cooks evenly. Remove from the heat and let the mix cool to room temperature, and then chill completely in the refrigerator.

You can make the ice cream now, or for a fuller and more developed flavor, cover and let the mix rest overnight in the refrigerator. Before making the ice cream, remove three-fourths of the coffee beans with a slotted spoon. I like to leave some in because it's fun to get a few coffee beans in a scoop of the ice cream. If this doesn't appeal to you, remove all of the beans. Add the corn syrup and then pour the mix into an ice cream maker and process according to the manufacturer's instructions.

Scoop the ice cream into a container and then place in the freezer to cure and harden. You are going to end up with a very full-flavored and creamy coffee ice cream that you will love. *Makes 8 servings.*

○ coffee and caramel swirl ○

This also is wonderful using Hot Fudge Sauce (page 120) or Chocolate Sauce (page 119). Just make sure that the sauces are cool before swirling them into the ice cream.

homemade version

1 recipe Shot of Coffee ice cream
  (page 38)
⅔ cup Caramel Sauce (page 121)

Make the Shot of Coffee ice cream according to directions. After the mix has been processed, scoop it into a chilled bowl and drizzle on the Caramel Sauce. Swirl it into the ice cream a little with a rubber spatula, but don't blend it all the way in. You want distinct swirls of caramel throughout the ice cream. Put in a container and then place in the freezer to cure and harden. *Makes 8 servings.*

easy mix-in version

Replace the Shot of Coffee ice cream with 1 quart premium store-bought coffee ice cream. Soften the ice cream and place in a medium-size mixing bowl. Drizzle on the Caramel Sauce. Swirl it into the ice cream a little with a rubber spatula, but don't blend it all the way in. You want distinct swirls of caramel through the ice cream. Return ice cream to container and put in freezer to cure and harden.

○ double espresso ○

This is a pumped-up version of the Shot of Coffee.

homemade version

1 recipe Shot of Coffee ice cream
  (page 38)
1 double espresso

Make the Shot of Coffee ice cream according to directions. When you pour the mix into the ice cream maker to process, add the double espresso. Process the ice cream according to the manufacturer's instructions. Place the ice cream in a container and then in the freezer to cure and harden. *Makes 8 servings.*

easy mix-in version

Replace the Shot of Coffee ice cream with 1 quart premium store-bought coffee ice cream. Soften the ice cream and place in a medium-size mixing bowl. Fold in the double espresso. Return ice cream to container and put in freezer to cure and harden.

° new orleans coffee °

I love this ice cream, and it's so easy to make! It has many layers of flavors and is an all-time favorite of our clientele.

homemade version

1 recipe Shot of Coffee ice cream
  (page 38)
2 tablespoons bourbon (I like Van
  Winkles 12 year)
5 tablespoons dark brown sugar
½ cup chopped and lightly
  toasted pecans

Make the Shot of Coffee ice cream according to directions. When you pour the mix into the ice cream maker to process, add the bourbon. Process the ice cream according to the manufacturer's instructions. When it is done, scoop it into a chilled bowl and fold in the brown sugar and the pecans. Place the ice cream in a container and then in the freezer to cure and harden. *Makes 8 servings.*

easy mix-in version

Replace the Shot of Coffee ice cream with 1 quart premium store-bought coffee ice cream. Soften the ice cream and place in a medium-size mixing bowl. Fold the whiskey, brown sugar, and pecans into the softened ice cream. Return ice cream to container and put in freezer to cure and harden.

∘ coffee, cookies, and cream ∘

This recipe adds a little playfulness to regular coffee ice cream.

homemade version

1 recipe Shot of Coffee ice cream
(page 38)
16 to 20 Oreo cookies, chopped

Make the Shot of Coffee ice cream according to directions. After the mix has been processed, scoop it into a chilled bowl and fold in the chopped Oreo cookies (or any other chopped cookie that you like). Place the ice cream in a container and then in the freezer to cure and harden. *Makes 8 servings.*

easy mix-in version

Replace the Shot of Coffee ice cream with 1 quart premium store-bought coffee ice cream. Soften the ice cream and place in a medium-size mixing bowl. Fold in the chopped Oreo cookies. Return ice cream to container and put in freezer to cure and harden.

° mocha hot cocoa °

I love a good Mocha drink on a freezing day, and we have a lot of those up here in the mountains. A mocha is a drink of hot cocoa and espresso, and this is my ice cream version of the drink.

1 recipe Double Espresso ice cream (page 40)

1 cup good-quality milk chocolate cocoa mix

Make the Double Espresso ice cream according to directions, adding in the cocoa mix during the cooking process. Chill the mix and process the ice cream according to the manufacturer's instructions. Place ice cream in a container and then into the freezer to cure and harden. This ice cream is mellow with an edge and is good on any kind of day. *Makes 8 servings.*

○ italian coffee ○

I call this coffee ice cream Italian because we add almond extract, and that gives it an Italian touch.

homemade version

1 recipe Shot of Coffee ice cream (page 38) or Double Espresso ice cream (page 40)

1 teaspoon pure almond extract

½ cup slivered almonds, toasted to a golden brown

½ cup Caramel Sauce (page 121) or Chocolate Sauce (page 119)

Make the Shot of Coffee ice cream or Double Espresso ice cream according to directions. When you pour the mix into the ice cream maker to process, add the almond extract. When it is done, scoop it into a chilled bowl and sprinkle on the slivered almonds and then drizzle on the sauce. Swirl it into the ice cream a little with a rubber spatula, but don't blend it all the way in. You want distinct swirls of caramel (or chocolate) and almonds throughout the ice cream. Place ice cream in a container and then into the freezer to cure and harden. *Makes 1½ quarts.*

easy mix-in version

Replace the Shot of Coffee or Double Espresso ice cream with 1 quart premium store-bought coffee ice cream. Soften the ice cream and place in a medium-size mixing bowl. Fold in the almond extract, and then sprinkle on the slivered almonds. Drizzle on the sauce. Swirl it into the ice cream a little with a rubber spatula, but don't blend it all the way in. You want distinct swirls of caramel (or chocolate) and almonds throughout the ice cream. Return ice cream to container and put in freezer to cure and harden.

crème brûlée
ice creams

I've always loved the dessert known as Crème Brûlée—a light, creamy custard with a burnt sugar crust. Burnt sugar gives the ice cream that wonderful caramelized flavor.

On a special note, here is a fun idea you can try with any of these ice creams. When the ice cream is finished processing in the ice cream maker, spoon it into a chilled bowl. Pour over it ⅓ cup Caramel Sauce (page 121), Chocolate Sauce (page 119), or Hot Fudge Sauce (page 120).

With a large spoon or rubber spatula, fold the sauce into the ice cream, making swirls. Don't blend it all the way in—you just want to fold it a few times to make nice swirls. Quickly put the ice cream into the freezer to cure and harden. Also, try a combination using ⅓ cup of each sauce for an extra special treat. Note: Make sure the sauce you use is cool before folding it in because you don't want it to melt the ice cream.

◦ crème brûlée ◦

This is the standard crème brûlée ice cream recipe. Serve it plain or build on it for other variations.

2 cups whipping cream
2 cups whole milk
1½ cups sugar, divided
2 tablespoons pure vanilla extract
6 egg yolks
2 tablespoons water
½ cup light corn syrup, optional

Pour the cream and milk into a medium-size stainless steel bowl and place over a steaming pan of boiling water. When the mix gets hot, a film will form over the surface. Add ½ cup sugar, vanilla, and egg yolks. Stir the mix with a wire whip and make sure all of the ingredients are blended together.

While the mixture is cooking, put 1 cup sugar into a saucepan and add the water. Over medium-high heat, caramelize the sugar. The sugar will dissolve in the water and then begin to burn. Stir it with a wire whip so it cooks evenly and let it caramelize to a nice rich brown color. The caramelized sugar is very hot so be careful. Use a towel or kitchen gloves and pour the sugar mixture into the ice cream mix. Be careful because it will splatter, so stand back a little. Stir the mixture until everything is well blended; let steep a few minutes more, stirring occasionally. Add the corn syrup if using. (This helps give the ice cream a wonderful scoopable texture. Try it both ways and see what way you like best. As always, I encourage you to experiment and try your own ideas.)

Remove from the heat and let the mix cool to room temperature and then chill completely in the refrigerator. Pour the mix into an ice cream maker and process according to the manufacturer's instructions. Scoop the ice cream into a container and then place in the freezer to cure and harden. *Makes 8 servings.*

∘ toasted pecan brûlée ∘

Toasted nuts go so well with this ice cream!

homemade version

*1 recipe Crème Brûlée ice cream
  (page 50)*

*1 cup chopped pecans, toasted
  and cooled*

Make the Crème Brûlée ice cream according to directions. A few minutes before the ice cream comes out of the ice cream maker, pour in the pecans. When ice cream is finished processing, scoop into a container and then place in the freezer to cure and harden. *Makes 8 servings.*

easy mix-in version

Replace the Crème Brûlée ice cream with 1 quart premium store-bought crème brûlée ice cream. Soften the ice cream and place in a medium-size mixing bowl. Fold the pecans into the softened ice cream. Return ice cream to container and put in freezer to cure and harden.

○ new orleans crème brûlée ○

This is the essence of New Orleans.

1 recipe Crème Brûlée ice cream
  (page 50)
1 cup chopped pecans, toasted
  and cooled
1 tablespoon brown sugar
2 tablespoons good bourbon
  or brandy

Make the Crème Brûlée ice cream according to directions. After the mix has been processed, scoop it into a chilled bowl and then fold in the pecans, brown sugar, and bourbon whiskey or brandy. Put in a container and then place in the freezer to cure and harden. *Makes 8 servings.*

macadamia nut brûlée

For an exotic taste, dress up Crème Brûlée ice cream with toasted macadamia nuts.

homemade version

*1 recipe Crème Brûlée ice cream
  (page 50)*
*1 cup chopped macadamia nuts,
  lightly toasted and cooled*

Make the Crème Brûlée ice cream according to directions. A few minutes before the ice cream comes out of the ice cream maker, pour in the macadamia nuts. When done, scoop into a container and then place in the freezer to cure and harden. *Makes 8 servings.*

easy mix-in version

Replace the Crème Brûlée ice cream with 1 quart premium store-bought crème brûlée ice cream. Soften the ice cream and place in a medium-size mixing bowl. Fold the macadamia nuts into the softened ice cream. Return ice cream to container and put in freezer to cure and harden.

○ burnt orange brûlée ○

I got the idea for this ice cream after John Prine came out with his album called "Burnt Orange," which I loved.

homemade version

1 recipe Crème Brûlée ice cream
(page 50)
Zest of 1 large orange

Make the Crème Brûlée ice cream according to directions. Stir the zest into the mix as it is cooking. This will impart an orange flavor that is delicious. When done cooking, remove from the heat, let cool to room temperature, and then chill completely in the refrigerator. Pour the mix into an ice cream maker and process according to the manufacturer's instructions. Scoop the ice cream into a container and then place in the freezer to cure and harden. *Makes 8 servings.*

easy mix-in version

Replace the Crème Brûlée ice cream with 1 quart premium store-bought crème brûlée ice cream. Soften the ice cream and place in a medium-size mixing bowl. Fold the orange zest into the softened ice cream. Return ice cream to container and put in freezer to cure and harden.

∘ peanut butter cookies
and cream brûlée ∘

Here is a sophisticated and slightly wild version of Crème Brûlée ice cream. Peanut butter cookies taste great with this ice cream, so why not fold some in to make peanut butter cookies and cream brûlée?

homemade version

1 recipe Crème Brûlée ice cream
  (page 50)
10 to 14 peanut butter cookies,
  chopped

Make the crème brûlée ice cream according to directions. After the ice cream is done processing, remove it from the ice cream maker and place in a large bowl. Fold in the chopped cookies. Then scoop ice cream into a container and place in the freezer to cure and harden. *Makes 8 servings.*

easy mix-in version

Replace the Crème Brûlée ice cream with 1 quart premium store-bought crème brûlée ice cream. Soften the ice cream and place in a medium-size mixing bowl. Fold the chopped cookies into the softened ice cream. Return ice cream to container and put in freezer to cure and harden.

sorbets

My wife, Sheila, and I were at an ice cream stand under the Eiffel Tower in Paris one afternoon sampling ice creams and sorbets. They all had that special magic and surprise that make some things so good. The sorbets seemed as creamy and smooth as the ice creams, and I wondered how they did it, considering there is no cream in sorbet.

The experience sent me on a personal quest to find the answer to my question. How could sorbet be so smooth and creamy with such a distinctive flavor of the fruit? I had had many sorbets before the trip to France, and, frankly, they weren't that good. They could be icy, grainy, and not exactly bursting with flavor. So how did they do it? What was the secret?

Well I think I found the answer, and it is really three elements. The first is obvious—good ripe fruit that is in season. There is no substitute for it! The second element is that there must be an acid ingredient in the sorbet to play off the sweetness of the ripe fruit, otherwise the sorbet would be cloyingly sweet. Lemons and limes are the answer. The third element, and maybe the most basic to the sorbet as it is the foundation, is the simple syrup—a mixture of sugar and water that is cooked for a few minutes. It's all about chemistry. The combination of all these elements brings about a structure that leads to smooth and creamy sorbet.

As a final note, be creative and substitute just about any fresh fruit you like into these recipes. By simply substituting fruits like pineapple, raspberries, papayas, or peaches, making them into fresh purees, and then following the basic recipes, you will have a wealth of sorbet flavors at your command.

○ simple syrup ○

This is the simple syrup that the French use, a very potent and unapologetic mixture of water and sugar that allows sorbet makers to use more fruit to attain the intense flavor of the sorbets and at the same time allows the sorbets to be smooth and creamy.

2 cups sugar

1 cup water

Combine the sugar and the water in a saucepan. Bring to a boil and then reduce heat to a low boil and cook for 1 minute. Remove from heat and cool down; reserve until you are ready to make the sorbet. You can make bigger batches if you are making lots of sorbet, just remember to always follow the proportions of two parts sugar to one part water.

○ fresh pear sorbet ○

This is one of my favorite sorbets because we usually have the best pears available all winter. The Oregon crop of pears is harvested all the way through late fall, and this allows us to make a delicious fresh fruit sorbet in the middle of winter; that goes over big-time up here in the mountains of Sun Valley.

5 or 6 ripe pears, peeled, cored,
  and cut into pieces
1 or 2 lemons
2 cups cooled Simple Syrup
  (page 60)

Put the pears in a food processor and puree. You'll need about 3¾ cups puree. Squeeze enough lemons to make ¼ cup lemon juice. Mix together the Simple Syrup, lemon juice, and pear puree. Pour the mix into an ice cream maker and process according to the manufacturer's instructions. When done, scoop into a container and then place in the freezer to cure and harden. You'll be amazed at the intense pear flavor of this sorbet. *Makes 6 to 8 servings.*

○ fresh mango sorbet ○

For a tropical touch, try this fresh mango sorbet. It tastes wonderful and is so good for you that you cannot go wrong.

5 to 7 very ripe mangoes, peeled,
*   seeded, and cut into pieces*
3 to 4 limes
2 cups cooled Simple Syrup
*   (page 60)*

Put the mangoes in a food processor and puree. You'll need about 3¾ cups puree. Squeeze enough limes to make ¼ cup lime juice. Mix together the Simple Syrup, lime juice, and mango puree. Pour mix into an ice cream maker and process according to the manufacturer's instructions. When done, scoop into a container and then place in the freezer to cure and harden. *Makes 6 to 8 servings.*

◦ strawberry sorbet ◦

Make this sorbet only when the strawberries are absolutely ripe and sweet.
Strawberries from your own garden or a u-pick truck farm are the best, and organic
is even better as this sorbet is fresh raw food. You don't want anything to contaminate
the ingredients! You want to know that what you are eating is fresh and pure and
healthy. I believe this is true with all food, and strawberry sorbet is a good place to
start applying this principle.

*1½ to 2 pounds strawberries,
washed, dried, and stemmed*

1 or 2 lemons

*2 cups cooled Simple Syrup
(page 60)*

Put the strawberries in a food processor and puree. You'll need about
3¾ cups puree. Squeeze enough lemons to make ¼ cup lemon juice.
Mix together the Simple Syrup, lemon juice, and strawberry puree.
Pour mix into an ice cream maker and process according to the
manufacturer's instructions. When done, scoop into a container and
then place in the freezer to cure and harden. *Makes 6 to 8 servings.*

sorbets

○ satsuma mandarin sorbet ○

Satsuma mandarins are always available late fall, and we continue to have them available through the Christmas holiday season as well. It is a tradition of mine to serve this sorbet over the holiday season at my restaurant. But when the Satsuma go out of season, you can continue to make great orange and tangerine sorbets simply by substituting freshly squeezed orange juice or blood orange juice or any other variety of tangerine so you can have this delicious citrus sorbet year-round.

1 or 2 lemons
3¾ cups freshly squeezed
Satsuma mandarin juice (12 to 15
mandarins)
2 cups cooled Simple Syrup
(page 60)

Squeeze enough lemons to make ¼ cup lemon juice. Combine lemon juice, Satsuma mandarin juice, and Simple Syrup; pour the mix into an ice cream maker and process according to the manufacturer's instructions. When done, scoop into a container and then place in the freezer to cure and harden. *Makes 6 to 8 servings.*

○ kiwi lime sorbet ○

This sorbet is my homage to the South Pacific and New Zealand. Kiwifruit add a lovely texture to the sorbet that is just a little unique. This sorbet is for all of my buddies down in the southern hemisphere.

8 to 10 kiwifruit, peeled and sliced
¾ cup freshly squeezed orange
   juice
¼ cup freshly squeezed lime juice
2 cups cooled Simple Syrup
   (page 60)

Place the kiwifruit in a food processor and puree. You will need about 3¾ cups puree. Mix together the Simple Syrup, orange and lime juice, and puree. Pour mix into an ice cream maker and process according to the manufacturer's instructions. When done, scoop into a container and then place in the freezer to cure and harden. *Makes 8 to 10 servings.*

◦ lemon sorbet ◦

This is a really feisty sorbet because lemons are so potent. We tame it down just enough by using a little less lemon juice and adding a little orange juice. For a real lemon rush, this is your sorbet!

*3 cups freshly squeezed lemon
  juice (8 to 10 lemons)*
*1 cup freshly squeezed orange
  juice (2 to 3 oranges)*
*2 cups cooled Simple Syrup
  (page 60)*

Combine all of the ingredients and then pour the mix into an ice cream maker. Process according to the manufacturer's instructions. When done, scoop into a container and then place in the freezer to cure and harden. *Makes 6 to 8 servings.*

° cassis sorbet °

I think of Cassis sorbet as the quintessential French sorbet. You see it in bistros all around France and it is simply one of those flavors that is part of the French culture. Cassis is the juice of the black currant berry, and I have found it available in a concentrated form imported from France in gourmet specialty shops or online. So if you are inclined, like I am, to have a little taste of the French culture once in a while, make the effort to find a source of cassis. You won't regret it.

3⅞ cups concentrated cassis juice

2 tablespoons freshly squeezed
  lemon juice

2 cups cooled Simple Syrup
  (page 60)

Combine all of the ingredients and then pour the mix into an ice cream maker. Process according to the manufacturer's instructions. When done, scoop into a container and then place in the freezer to cure and harden. *Makes 6 to 8 servings.*

ice creams
around the world

There's nothing like taking a trip around the world through the food you create right in your own kitchen, and with ice cream it's no exception. You literally can create the tastes of far-off places and exotic regions of the world in the ice creams that you make. So let's go on a trip to southern France or Morocco or Jamaica. How about Italy or China or the South Pacific? Are you with me?

∘ crème fraîche ∘

Crème fraîche is the cultured heavy cream of France. It is rich, slightly cheesy, and has a delicious tartness to it that explodes in your mouth. It is very easy to make crème fraîche. It makes unreal ice cream, but you can also use it to spoon over berries or peaches and sprinkle with a little sugar, or use it to enliven a sauce.

1 cup cultured buttermilk
4 cups whipping cream
5 ultra pasteurized egg yolks
¾ cup of sugar
½ cup light corn syrup

To make the crème fraîche, mix the buttermilk with the cream. Put the mixture into a clean wine carafe or glass container, cover it with plastic wrap, and let it sit out at room temperature overnight. The cream will thicken up a lot, like yogurt. The next day put the carafe in the refrigerator for two days to let the flavors develop and become thick and tart.

To make the ice cream, beat the egg yolks and sugar with a wire whip for a few minutes until they turn a creamy yellow color. Add the crème fraîche and the rest of the ingredients and blend thoroughly. Pour into an ice cream maker and process according to the manufacturer's instructions. Scoop the ice cream into a container and then place in the freezer to cure and harden. *Makes 6 to 8 servings.*

Note: This is an uncooked ice cream mixture, so use ultra pasteurized egg yolks. Ask your grocer to order you some.

∘ coconut ∘

This is a luscious ice cream from the Caribbean.

1 can (15 ounces) Coco Lopez
   cream of coconut
¾ can whipping cream
½ can whole milk
⅔ cup lightly toasted sweetened
   coconut flakes

Pour Coco Lopez into a medium-size stainless steel mixing bowl. If the coconut cream is really thick, put it over a steaming pan of water so it melts to an even consistency, but don't let it get too warm. Using the empty Coco Lopez can, first measure ¾ can of whipping cream and add to the coconut cream, then ½ can of milk and add into the coconut cream. Stir to blend. Pour the mix into an ice cream maker and process according to the manufacturer's instructions. Just before the ice cream is finished processing, add the coconut flakes. Scoop the ice cream into a container and then place in the freezer to cure and harden. *Makes 6 to 8 servings.*

° tamarind °

Tamarind is a fruit that comes from India. The fruit of the tamarind is a large pod with a reddish-brown pulpy flesh and large hard seeds. It's a little difficult and time consuming to deal with, but luckily it is available in a natural tamarind concentrate in the Asian section of many grocery stores. The tamarind concentrate makes a very good and exotic ice cream when mixed with coconut ice cream. It is sweet and tart, and is a unique ice cream with an exotic flavor from another world.

1 recipe Coconut ice cream, minus the coconut flakes (page 73)
10 ounces natural tamarind concentrate

Make the Coconut ice cream according to directions, except eliminate the coconut flakes. When you pour the mix into the ice cream maker to process, add the tamarind concentrate. Process the ice cream according to the manufacturer's instructions. Place the ice cream in a container and then in the freezer to cure and harden. *Makes 6 to 8 servings.*

Left to right: Strawberry Sorbet (page 64),
Crème Fraîche (page 72), and Tamarind.

∘ ambrosia ∘

Do you remember the dessert ambrosia? Pineapple, mandarin oranges, banana, coconut, sour cream, whipped cream, powdered sugar, dates, and nuts. That's ambrosia. It came to me that my Coconut ice cream would make a great foundation for an ambrosia ice cream. And here it is.

homemade version

1 recipe Coconut ice cream
  (page 73)
½ cup chopped and lightly toasted
  walnuts or pecans
½ cup cherry preserves
½ cup pineapple preserves

Make the Coconut ice cream according to directions. After the mix has been processed, scoop it into a chilled bowl and fold in the nuts and the preserves. Do not blend in thoroughly, as you want the preserves to form distinctive swirls. Scoop the ice cream into a container and then place in the freezer to cure and harden. *Makes 6 to 8 servings.*

easy mix-in version

1 quart premium store-bought
  coconut pineapple ice cream
½ cup chopped and lightly toasted
  walnuts or pecans
½ cup cherry preserves
½ cup pineapple preserves

Soften the ice cream and place in a medium-size mixing bowl. Fold in the nuts. Swirl in the preserves with a little rubber spatula. Do not blend in thoroughly, as you want the preserves to form distinctive swirls. Return ice cream to container and put in freezer to cure and harden.

° green tea °

Here is a surprising ice cream from Japan. I love it. It's unique, different, and easy to make.

2 cups whipping cream

2 cups whole milk

2 heaping tablespoons Japanese-grown green tea leaves

1 teaspoon ground ginger powder

1 cup sugar

1 drop green food coloring (optional)

Pour the cream and milk into a medium-size stainless steel bowl and place over a steaming pan of boiling water. When the mix gets hot, a film will form over the surface.

Add the remaining ingredients and let the mixture steep over the heat for about 10 minutes. Remove from the heat and let the mix cool to room temperature, and then chill completely in the refrigerator. Strain out most or all of the green tea leaves before making the ice cream. Pour the mix into an ice cream maker and process according to the manufacturer's instructions. Scoop the ice cream into a container and then place in the freezer to cure and harden. *Makes 6 to 8 servings.*

Dessert suggestion: Serve 2 small scoops of Green Tea ice cream per person and pour 1 tablespoon good sake over each portion. Sprinkle the ice cream with thin slivers of crystallized ginger. It's very simple, very Asian, and very refreshing. A great way to complete a visit to the Far East!

○ untamed ginger ○

This is full blast ginger ice cream. It's hot and sweet, not to mention wild—one of my favorite states of being! It's an instant cure for both body and soul. So hang on and give it a shot!

ginger simple syrup

1 cup water

1½ cups sugar

1 cup slivered crystallized ginger

ice cream

2 cups whipping cream

2 cups whole milk

1 cup sugar

4 ounces thinly sliced peeled fresh gingerroot

1 teaspoon Chinese ground ginger powder

7 fresh egg yolks

To make the Ginger Simple Syrup, combine the water, sugar, and crystallized ginger in a saucepan; bring to a boil and then turn down the heat and simmer the mixture for 10 minutes. Set aside.

Meanwhile, pour the cream and milk into a medium-size stainless steel bowl and place over a steaming pan of boiling water. When the mix gets hot, a film will form over the surface.

Add the sugar, gingerroot, and ginger powder; let cook for about 7 minutes. Stir in the egg yolks with a wire whip until thoroughly incorporated; let steep for 10 minutes while stirring occasionally so it cooks evenly. Remove from the heat and let the mix cool to room temperature, and then chill completely in the refrigerator. The ginger flavor will really develop as the mix cools down.

Remove the ginger slices with a slotted spoon and then add 1 cup Ginger Simple Syrup to the ice cream mix and blend it in thoroughly. Pour the mix into an ice cream maker and process according to the manufacturer's instructions. Scoop the ice cream into a container and then place in the freezer to cure and harden. *Makes 6 to 8 servings.*

Note: To let the ginger flavor develop even more, cover the mix and leave it in the refrigerator overnight and then make the ice cream the next day.

° jasmine °

Chinese Jasmine tea makes very good ice cream. I like to steep the mixture with a little chopped lemon grass to give it some complexity and citrus overtones. I hope you'll try this ice cream.

2 cups whipping cream

2 cups whole milk

2 heaping tablespoons Chinese
    Jasmine tea leaves

½ teaspoon Chinese ground
    ginger powder

2 tablespoons chopped
    lemon grass

1 cup sugar

Pour the cream and milk into a medium-size stainless steel bowl and place over a steaming pan of boiling water. When the mix gets hot, a film will form over the surface.

Stir in the remaining ingredients and let steep for 10 minutes. Remove from the heat and let the mix cool to room temperature, and then chill completely in the refrigerator. Strain out most or all of the jasmine tea leaves before making the ice cream. Pour the mix into an ice cream maker and process according to the manufacturer's instructions. Scoop the ice cream into a container and then place in the freezer to cure and harden. *Makes 8 to 10 servings.*

Dessert suggestion: Serve with Chinese almond cookies and a drizzle of homemade honey rum syrup. Simply melt 2 tablespoons light-colored honey with 2 tablespoons light rum. This makes enough syrup to drizzle over 4 servings of ice cream.

◦ honey saffron ◦

This one transports you to the heady street markets of Morocco.

homemade version

1 cup whipping cream

3 cups whole milk

¾ cups sugar, divided

½ cup orange blossom honey

Pinch of saffron

1 tablespoon pure vanilla extract

10 fresh egg yolks

Pour the cream and milk into a medium-size stainless steel bowl and place over a steaming pan of boiling water. When the mix gets hot, a film will form over the surface.

Add half the sugar and the honey, saffron, and vanilla. In another bowl, beat the egg yolks with the remaining sugar for about 2 minutes. Stir the egg yolk mixture into the hot cream mix; stir until it thickens, about 5 to 7 minutes. Remove from the heat and let the mix cool to room temperature, and then chill completely in the refrigerator.

Pour the mix into an ice cream maker and process according to the manufacturer's instructions. Scoop the ice cream into a container and then place in the freezer to cure and harden. *Makes 6 to 8 servings.*

easy mix-in version

1 quart premium
 vanilla ice cream

¼ cup orange blossom honey

Pinch of saffron

1 tablespoon pure vanilla extract

Soften the ice cream and place in a medium-size mixing bowl. Fold in the honey, saffron, and vanilla. Return ice cream to container and put in freezer to cure and harden.

º french lavender º

This ice cream is from the hot hills of Provence in southern France, where lavender grows on the hillsides overlooking the Mediterranean Sea. The recipe is inspired by one of my favorite French chefs and a mentor from afar, Roger Verge.

1½ cups sugar

1 tablespoon + 1 teaspoon whole dried lavender flowers, divided

8 ultra pasteurized egg yolks

1½ cups whipping cream

1½ cups whole milk

½ cup sour cream

1 tablespoon pure vanilla extract

Put the sugar in a blender with 1 tablespoon lavender and grind the mixture until you have lavender sugar. This only takes a few seconds. Put the egg yolks into a stainless steel bowl and add the lavender sugar. With a wire whip, beat the mixture until the sugar, is well blended into the yolks and the mix turns a nice pale yellow color. This takes a few minutes.

Now add the cream, milk, sour cream, and vanilla. Whip the mixture until well blended. Stir in 1 teaspoon dried lavender flowers. Process in an ice cream maker according to the manufacturer's instructions. Scoop the ice cream into a container and then place in the freezer to cure and harden. *Makes 8 to 10 servings.*

Note: This is an uncooked ice cream mixture, so use ultra pasteurized egg yolks. Ask your grocer to order you some.

ice creams around the world

∘ fresh basil ∘

You've got to love the French, as they have no boundaries when it comes to food. Here is a great example of that.

1 cup whipping cream

2 cups whole milk

3 ounces fresh basil leaves, chopped

1 cup sugar

6 fresh egg yolks

1 teaspoon pure vanilla extract

¼ cup light honey (orange blossom works well)

Pour the cream, milk, and basil into a medium-size stainless steel bowl and place over a steaming pan of boiling water. When the mix gets hot, a film will form over the surface.

Continue heating for about 10 to 15 minutes. This will bring out the basil flavor and infuse it into the cream. Stir the mix now and then to distribute the flavor. In a second bowl, put the sugar, egg yolks, and vanilla and beat with a wire whip until the mixture turns a very nice pale yellow color and is smooth, about 2 minutes. Add the sugar mixture to the cream mixture and blend together thoroughly. Cook over the steaming water for about 5 minutes more. Add the honey and blend. Strain the mixture to remove the cooked basil and remove from heat.

Chill completely in the refrigerator before pouring into an ice cream maker. Process according to the manufacturer's instructions. Scoop the ice cream into a container and then place in the freezer to cure and harden. *Makes 8 to 10 servings.*

° fresh rosemary °

Here is another fresh herb ice cream. Think Greece. Imagine bees buzzing around a rosemary hillside on an island overlooking the Aegean Sea. Be transported. That's what it is all about.

⅓ cup coarsely chopped fresh rosemary leaves

1 cup whipping cream

2 cups whole milk

6 fresh egg yolks

1 cup sugar

1 teaspoon finely grated lemon zest

1 teaspoon pure vanilla extract

¼ cup light honey (orange blossom works well)

Take the coarsely chopped rosemary and mash it up a little so the flavor is released. Pour the cream, milk, and rosemary into a medium-size stainless steel bowl and place over a steaming pan of boiling water. When the mix gets hot, a film will form over the surface. Continue heating for 10 to 15 minutes to bring out the flavor of the rosemary.

In a separate bowl, add the egg yolks, sugar, lemon zest, and vanilla, and beat with a wire whip until the sugar dissolves into the yolks and the mix turns a nice pale yellow color and is smooth, about 2 minutes. Add the sugar mixture to the cream mixture, stirring constantly to blend thoroughly. Continue cooking the mix for about 5 minutes more. Add the honey and blend. Strain the mix to remove the rosemary leaves. (I like to add back into the mix a very small amount of the rosemary leaves just for effect.)

Chill completely in the refrigerator before pouring into an ice cream maker. Process according to the manufacturer's instructions. Scoop the ice cream into a container and then place in the freezer to cure and harden. *Makes 8 to 10 servings.*

° red rose petal °

This is a beautiful rosy ice cream that tastes like you're walking through a rose garden.

1½ cups sugar

*3 tablespoons crushed dried red
  rose petals, divided*

8 ultra pasteurized egg yolks

1½ cups whipping cream

1½ cups whole milk

½ cup sour cream

1 tablespoon pure vanilla extract

Put the sugar into a blender with 2 tablespoons rose petals and grind the mixture for a few seconds. You now have rose petal sugar. Put the egg yolks into a bowl and add the rose sugar; beat the mixture until the sugar dissolves into the yolks and the mix turns a pale rosy color. This takes a couple of minutes.

Add the cream, milk, sour cream, and vanilla. Whip the mixture until everything is well blended. Add the extra tablespoon of rose petals and then pour into an ice cream maker and process according to the manufacturer's instructions. Scoop the ice cream into a container and then place in the freezer to cure and harden. *Makes 8 to 10 servings.*

Note: This is an uncooked ice cream mixture, so use ultra pasteurized egg yolks. Ask your grocer to order you some.

∘ fresh peach ∘

If you have homegrown peaches, there is nothing better than this ice cream. This is one of the first ice creams I was introduced to by my grandfather, Clint, way back when. Ripe fruit is the key.

homemade version

1½ pounds ripe peaches, peeled
and pitted and cut into pieces
1 cup sugar, divided
1 cup whipping cream
1 cup whole milk
2 tablespoons freshly squeezed
lemon juice

Toss the peaches and ¼ cup sugar in a bowl and let macerate for 1 hour. Put the peaches into a food processor and puree. Combine the cream, milk, remaining sugar, and peach puree in a bowl. Pour the mix into an ice cream maker, add the lemon juice, and process according to the manufacturer's instructions. Scoop it into a container and then place in the freezer to cure and harden. *Makes 8 to 10 servings.*

Note: This recipe can be made with whatever fruit strikes your fancy. Simply follow the recipe and substitute any fruit you love.

easy mix-in version

1½ pounds ripe peaches, peeled
and pitted and cut into pieces
¼ cup sugar
1 quart premium vanilla ice cream

Follow the instructions above for macerating and pureeing the peaches. Soften the ice cream and place in a medium-size mixing bowl. Fold in the pureed peaches; return ice cream to container and put in freezer to cure and harden.

° organic banana °

I love to make banana ice cream from overripe organic bananas. They seem to be richer and creamier than regular bananas. But if organic bananas are not available, use regular bananas, as they are good too. Just make sure the bananas are overripe, just like you would use for banana bread. Overripe bananas have a lot more flavor.

1½ cups whipping cream
1½ cups whole milk
1 cup sugar
¼ cup orange blossom honey
2 tablespoons pure vanilla extract
8 egg yolks
8 overripe bananas
½ cup sour cream

Pour the cream and milk into a medium-size stainless steel bowl and place over a steaming pan of boiling water. When the mix gets hot, a film will form over the surface.

Add the sugar, honey, vanilla, and egg yolks and blend evenly; let steep for about 7 minutes. Remove from the heat and let the mix cool to room temperature, and then chill completely in the refrigerator. In small batches, process the cream mixture with the bananas and the sour cream in a food processor. When done, pour the mix into an ice cream maker and process according to the manufacturer's instructions. Scoop the ice cream into a container and then place in the freezer to cure and harden.

The keys to good banana ice cream are not cooking the bananas in the mix so they taste fresh and using a little sour cream to add just a hint of tartness to the flavor profile. *Makes 12 to 16 servings.*

° perfect strawberry °

This strawberry ice cream contains no egg yolks and is uncooked and unheated. This allows the fruit to taste fresh and wonderful. So the key is to use the ripest, freshest fruit you can find. Make this ice cream with the fruit that is in season and use the best available. You'll be amazed at the flavor.

homemade version

1½ pounds fresh ripe strawberries, washed, dried, stemmed, and quartered

1 cup sugar, divided

1 cup whipping cream

1 cup whole milk

2 tablespoons freshly squeezed lemon juice

Toss the strawberries with ¼ cup sugar and let macerate for 1 hour. This brings on a chemistry change in the strawberries, develops the flavors, brings out the juices, and makes it bright and out front. Put the strawberries and their juices into a food processor and puree.

In a medium bowl add the cream, milk, remaining sugar, and strawberry puree and blend thoroughly. Pour the mix into an ice cream maker, add the lemon juice, and process according to the manufacturer's instructions. Scoop the ice cream into a container and then place in the freezer to cure and harden. *Makes 8 to 10 servings.*

easy mix-in version

1½ pounds fresh ripe strawberries, washed, dried, stemmed, and quartered

¼ cup sugar

1 quart premium vanilla ice cream

Follow the instructions above for macerating and pureeing the strawberries. Soften the ice cream and place in a medium-size mixing bowl. Fold in the pureed strawberries; return ice cream to container and put in freezer to cure and harden.

gelatos

Now we turn to Italy. Who's not ready for that? *Gelato* means ice cream in Italian. They make some of the best ice cream in the world. Bright flavors and super smooth texture. I love it. It's an interesting chemistry—less cream and more milk, lots more egg yolks. Whipping up the egg yolks and sugar to a mellow pale yellow ribbon before adding it to the cream mixture. That's what makes it so smooth. Let's make some gelato.

° vanilla bean gelato °

Real vanilla beans have a wonderful flavor that vanilla extract just doesn't do justice to.

homemade version

1 cup whipping cream

3 cups whole milk

4 vanilla beans

12 fresh egg yolks

1½ cups sugar

Pour the cream and milk into a medium-size stainless steel bowl and place over a steaming pan of boiling water. When the mix gets hot, a film will form over the surface.

Meanwhile, cut the vanilla beans in half lengthwise, scrape out the seeds, and then add the seeds and pods to the heating cream mixture. Allow the vanilla beans to steep in the hot cream for about 10 minutes. In another bowl, add the egg yolks and sugar, and beat until the mixture has turned to a nice pale yellow and is smooth, about 2 minutes. While stirring with the whip, add the sugar mixture to the hot cream mixture and thoroughly blend, cooking and stirring about 5 minutes. Remove from heat and chill completely in the refrigerator.

Using a slotted spoon, remove the bean pods before pouring the mix into an ice cream maker. Process according to the manufacturer's instructions. Scoop the ice cream into a container and then place in the freezer to cure and harden. *Makes 8 to 12 servings.*

easy mix-in version

As with my other vanilla ice creams, you can fold in extra ingredients to the gelato when it comes out of the ice cream maker. To make it really Italian, find Italian cookies you like, chop them up, and stir into the softened gelato to make an intense Italian cookies and cream gelato.

gelatos

∘ lemon gelato ∘

I am a lemon nut. So, for the creamiest of all lemon ice creams, try this Lemon Gelato, intensified by the wonderful Lemoncello, Italy's famous lemon liqueur.

1 cup whipping cream

3 cups whole milk

1½ cups sugar

12 fresh egg yolks

Zest of 1 medium lemon,
*   finely grated*

3 tablespoons Lemoncello

3 tablespoons freshly squeezed
*   lemon juice*

Pour the cream and milk into a medium-size stainless steel bowl and place over a steaming pan of boiling water. When the mix gets hot, a film will form over the surface.

In another bowl, add the sugar, egg yolks, lemon zest, and Lemoncello and beat with a wire whip until it's a pale yellow color and smooth, about 2 minutes. Add the sugar mixture to the hot cream mixture, stirring the whole time until well blended. Steep for about 5 minutes and then remove from the heat. Cool the mix completely in the refrigerator.

Add the fresh lemon juice just before pouring the mix into an ice cream maker. Process according to the manufacturer's instructions. Scoop the ice cream into a container and then place in the freezer to cure and harden. *Makes 8 to 12 servings.*

◦ italian coffee gelato ◦

In the spirit of the task at hand, you should make a second double espresso and drink it while preparing this ice cream!

1 cup whipping cream

3 cups whole milk

1 cup whole Italian roast
  coffee beans

1 tablespoon instant espresso
  powder (I like Madaglia D'Oro)

12 fresh egg yolks

1½ cups sugar

2 tablespoons pure vanilla extract

1 freshly made double espresso

Pour the cream and milk into a medium-size stainless steel bowl and place over a steaming pan of boiling water. When the mix gets hot, a film will form over the surface.

Add the coffee beans and espresso powder to the mix and let steep for 15 minutes. Meanwhile, in a separate bowl beat the egg yolks, sugar, and vanilla together until the mixture is a nice pale yellow and very smooth, about 2 minutes. Pour the sugar mixture in a thin stream gradually into the cream-and-coffee mix. Stir the mix constantly until well blended. Cook the mix about 5 minutes more. Blend in the freshly made double espresso.

Chill completely in the refrigerator. When ready to make the gelato, remove the whole beans with a slotted spoon and pour mix into an ice cream maker. Process according to the manufacturer's instructions. Scoop the ice cream into a container and then place in the freezer to cure and harden. *Makes 10 to 14 servings.*

Dessert suggestion: With each serving of Italian Coffee Gelato, top with a spoonful of fresh whipped cream and then sprinkle on a little cocoa powder, ground nutmeg, cinnamon, or freshly ground espresso. It's just like being in your favorite coffee bar.

gelatos

⚬ crème di marsala gelato ⚬

The best crème de marsala comes from Sicily. It is an old world flavor that you can enjoy with this gelato.

1 cup whipping cream
3 cups whole milk
12 fresh egg yolks
1 cup sugar
1 teaspoon pure vanilla extract
¾ cup crème de marsala,
 preferably Italian

Pour the cream and milk into a medium-size stainless steel bowl and place over a steaming pan of boiling water. When the mix gets hot, a film will form over the surface.

Meanwhile, in a separate bowl combine the egg yolks, sugar, and vanilla, and beat with a wire whip until it is a pale yellow color and smooth, about 2 minutes. In a thin stream, gradually pour the sugar mixture into the hot cream mixture, stirring until well blended. Cook the mix for about 5 minutes. Stir in the crème de marsala and cook about 5 minutes more, stirring every minute or so. Remove from heat to cool to room temperature and then place in the refrigerator to cool completely.

Pour mix into an ice cream maker and process according to the manufacturer's instructions. Scoop the ice cream into a container and then place in the freezer to cure and harden. *Makes 8 to 12 servings.*

Dessert suggestion: Serve a scoop of Crème de Marsala Gelato with a dollop of preserved purple plums in a splash of its own juice. It tastes amazing.

vanilla mascarpone gelato

Mascarpone is Italian cream cheese. It has a little sweetness and is a little creamier than American cream cheese. It makes a rich and delicious gelato that you will enjoy.

4 cups whole milk

12 fresh egg yolks

1 cup sugar

3 tablespoons pure vanilla extract

1½ teaspoons fresh grated lemon zest

1½ teaspoons fresh grated orange zest

8 ounces mascarpone

Pour the milk into a medium-size stainless steel bowl and place over a steaming pan of boiling water. When the mix gets hot, a film will form over the surface.

Meanwhile, in a separate bowl combine the egg yolks, sugar, vanilla, and zests. Beat mixture until it is a pale yellow color and smooth, about 2 minutes. Now in a light stream gradually pour the sugar mixture into the scalded milk, stirring with the wire whip to blend evenly. Cut up the mascarpone into small pieces and add it to the mix; stir until it is thoroughly blended into the mix. Continue stirring and cook the mix for about 5 minutes more.

Remove from heat to cool to room temperature and then place in the refrigerator to cool completely. Pour mix into an ice cream maker and process according to the manufacturer's instructions. Scoop the ice cream into a container and then place in the freezer to cure and harden. *Makes 12 to 14 servings.*

∘ frangelico mascarpone gelato ∘

This is where the fun really begins. Making these gelatos with your favorite liqueurs leads to endless possibilities of great times and maybe even romance! Good food is a form of romance anyway. This recipe is a good example. Frangelico is a hazelnut liqueur that combines in a heavenly way with cream and egg yolks and vanilla. It is unforgettable.

4 cups whole milk
1 cup sugar
12 fresh egg yolks
1 tablespoon pure vanilla extract
8 ounces mascarpone
1 cup Frangelico Liqueur

Pour the milk into a medium-size stainless steel bowl and place over a steaming pan of boiling water. When the mix gets hot, a film will form over the surface.

Meanwhile, in a separate bowl combine the sugar, egg yolks, and vanilla, and beat with a wire whip until it is a pale yellow color and smooth, about 2 minutes. In a light stream, gradually pour the sugar mixture into the scalded milk, stirring with the wire whip to blend evenly. Cut up the mascarpone into small pieces and add it to the mix, stirring until the cheese is blended in evenly.

Continue stirring and cooking the mixture for about 5 minutes more and then add the Frangelico, stirring until it is thoroughly blended into the mix. Cook about 2 minutes more and then remove from the heat. Cool completely in the refrigerator. Pour the mix into an ice cream maker and process according to the manufacturer's instructions. Scoop the ice cream into a container and then place in the freezer to cure and harden. *Makes 12 to 14 servings.*

Note: You can substitute amaretto or Grand Marnier for Frangelico.

gelatos

ice cream desserts

What I like in making ice cream desserts is the contrast of elements: temperature, texture, flavor. Ice cream is soft and creamy and cold, so I like to make desserts that have a crunchy element or a warm element or a fizzy element.

Ice cream goes well with marinated fruits and their juices, or grilled fruits flavored with brandy. Cookies and pastries combine very well with warm dessert sauces to make ice cream lush and sexy. Toasted nuts add a mouthwatering crunch.

These are some of the elements I use to make ice cream desserts with the kinds of contrasts I like. Some great recipes follow in this chapter. They are easy and fun and delicious. Give them a try and really enjoy what you create.

○ honey grilled peaches & ice cream ○

Fresh ripe peaches grilled with a heavenly coating of caramelized sugar and honey must be the essence of summer. Don't try this dish with out-of-season fruit. It just won't work.

4 ripe peaches, halves and pitted
2 tablespoons white sugar
8 teaspoons honey
4 teaspoons brandy or bourbon
4 scoops Crème Fraîche ice cream
  (page 72)

Put the peach halves in a bowl face up and sprinkle them with the sugar. Let macerate for 1 hour.

Very lightly oil the faces of the halved peaches and put them facedown on a medium-hot grill or barbecue. After 1 minute, turn each peach ¼ turn and cook 1 more minute. This will make nice crosshatch grill marks. Now turn the peaches over so the skin side is on the grill. Drizzle with the honey and the brandy or bourbon. Leave the peaches on the grill 1 or 2 more minutes.

Serve 2 peach halves with 1 scoop ice cream. Drizzle with Caramel Sauce if desired. *Makes 4 servings.*

∘ toasted pecan ice cream balls ∘

A great simple dessert. I love to coat scoops of ice cream with toasted nuts and serve them in a pool of Chocolate, Caramel, or Hot Fudge Sauce. Here is one of my favorite versions.

1 cup chopped toasted pecans
Hot Fudge Sauce (page 120)
8 small scoops White Chocolate
*   ice cream (page 36)*

Chop the pecans and toast them in an oven set at 350 degrees F for about 6 or 7 minutes. Cool them to room temperature. Warm up some Hot Fudge Sauce.

To serve, put the pecans in a large enough bowl to add a scoop of ice cream and roll it around in the nuts. Place one scoop at a time in the nuts, pressing it lightly into the nuts so they stick to the ice cream. Make a pool of 2 to 3 tablespoons of warmed Hot Fudge Sauce on each serving plate and place two of the pecan-coated ice cream balls in each pool. *Makes 4 servings.*

ice cream desserts

○ chimney sweeps gelato ○

This dessert is an eye-opener and is a true jolt to the soul.

2 scoops Vanilla Mascarpone
   Gelato (page 98)
4 tablespoons bourbon
Freshly ground espresso

Place each scoop of ice cream in a serving dish and pour 2 tablespoons bourbon over the top of each. Sprinkle with freshly ground espresso. *Makes 2 servings.*

° frozen ambrosia ice cream pie °

This is one of the many fun things you can do with ice cream that you won't find on the beaten path of regular ice cream desserts. It's related to that great old dessert that our moms used to make, ambrosia. Remember?

8 tablespoons unsalted butter, cut into pieces and at room temperature
2 tablespoons sour cream
2 tablespoons dark brown sugar
⅓ cup chopped dates
⅓ cup graham cracker crumbs
8 ounces chopped toasted pecans
Pinch sea salt
1 recipe Ambrosia ice cream, softened (page 76)

Put all of the ingredients except the ice cream into a food processor and process until everything is well blended and begins to clump together, about 10 seconds. Dump the crust mixture into a 9-inch pie pan and press the dough evenly over the entire pan.

Scoop the softened ice cream into the crust, mounding it up higher towards the center. Put the pie in the freezer for at least 3 hours and then serve when you are ready. Serve with warm Chocolate or Caramel Sauce (pages 119 and 121) drizzled over the top, or maybe even a dollop of whipped cream. *Makes 8 to 10 servings.*

° ice cream soufflés °

Ice cream soufflés are beautiful and bold presentations of ice cream that are creative and arty but are simple to make. Make them with whatever ice cream you like, whether it is homemade or premium store-bought ice cream. These have great presentation!

8 parchment paper sleeves
8 (3-ounce or 6-ounce) soufflé
  cups
1 quart ice cream of your choice
Fruit, chocolate, cookies, or edible
  flowers for garnish

Make the sleeves by wrapping parchment paper around each soufflé cup so that the sleeve extends 2 inches above the rim of the cup. Secure them with freezer tape or masking tape. Scoop softened ice cream into the soufflé cups and up to the top of the sleeve. Now refreeze the ice cream soufflés until ready to serve.

When you are ready to serve, take the frozen soufflés out of the freezer and remove the parchment paper. Garnish with fresh fruit, cookies, or shards of chocolate, or by pressing toasted coconut, jimmies, or edible flowers into the sides of the soufflés. Let your imagination run wild, and the results will dazzle your friends or family! *Makes 8 servings.*

• the world's best root beer float •

This dessert transports me back to my high school days at Anaheim High in Southern California, where in the fall after football practice on blistering hot days we'd drag ourselves across the street from the high school to the local A&W Root Beer Drive In. It was an old classic high school hangout. We would be bruised, tired, and thirsty, and nothing quenched my thirst more than an A&W Root Beer float. White chocolate ice cream and root beer make the best float of all!

1 frozen and frosted soda glass
1 can root beer (A&W for the
  authentic experience)
2 scoops White Chocolate ice
  cream (page 36)

Put the root beer into the frosted glass first. Add the ice cream. Let it rest a few seconds. Now dig in! *Makes 1 serving.*

∘ oreo cookie ice cream sandwiches ∘

These make really tasty little treats and are great for the kids or adults. You can substitute any kind of ice cream you like.

12 Oreo cookies
1 pint Creamy Milk Chocolate Malt
  ice cream (page 32) or Perfect
  Strawberry ice cream (page 92)

Remove ice cream from the freezer to soften. Separate the halves of each cookie. Leaving the Oreo filling intact, spoon some ice cream onto the bottom half of the cookie. I like to use enough ice cream to make the cookie about ½ inch thick. Now put the top half on and press down gently to form the cookie.

Put the ice cream sandwiches on a tray and place in the freezer for an hour or so, and then serve. *Makes 12 servings.*

° ginger snap ice cream sandwiches °

Find the very best ginger snap cookies that you can for this recipe—thin ones are best. Again, you can substitute whatever ice cream sounds best to you. Try different condiment combinations too. Be creative and have fun!

24 ginger snaps
1 to 2 pints Untamed Ginger ice
  cream (page 80) or Rich Vanilla
  ice cream (page 16)
Condiments (page 124)

Remove the ice cream from the freezer to soften. Spoon enough ice cream onto a cookie so that after you put a second cookie on top and press down, the sandwich is about $1/2$ to $3/4$ inch thick. Repeat for the remaining cookies to make a total of 12 sandwiches.

Roll the sides of the cookie in condiments such as finely grated chocolate, lightly toasted sweetened flaky coconut, or thinly sliced crystallized ginger. Put the ice cream sandwiches on a tray and place in the freezer for an hour or so, and then serve. Makes 12 servings.

∘ chocolate chip cookie
ice cream sandwiches ∘

These are a great all-American ice cream treat!

24 chocolate chip cookies
1 to 2 pints Rich Vanilla ice cream
  (page 16) or Philadelphia Vanilla
  Bean (page 14)

Remove ice cream from the freezer to soften. Spoon enough ice cream onto a cookie so that after you put a second cookie on top and press down, the sandwich is about ½ to ¾ inch thick. Repeat for the remaining cookies.

Put the ice cream sandwiches on a tray and place in the freezer for an hour or so, and then serve. *Makes 12 servings.*

ice cream desserts

○ asian wonton ice cream sandwiches ○

These are my favorite ice cream sandwiches. The wonton is crispy and is a great surprise with ice cream. What a great way to finish an Asian dinner party or a summer barbecue. Experiment with other ice creams, like Macadamia Nut Brûlée (page 54) or Tamarind (page 74). The possibilities are endless.

24 Wonton Cookies (page 123)
12 tablespoons Nutella
1 pint Coconut ice cream (page 73) or Untamed Ginger ice cream (page 80)
Chocolate Sauce (page 119)

Remove the ice cream from the freezer to soften. Spread 1 tablespoon Nutella evenly over a prepared crispy wonton cookie. Be careful when handling these cookies—they are fragile! Spoon enough ice cream onto a cookie so that after you put a second cookie on top and press down, the sandwich is about ½ to ¾ inch thick. Repeat for the remaining cookies.

Drizzle the sandwiches with chocolate sauce. Put them on a tray and place in the freezer for an hour or so, and then serve. *Makes 12 servings.*

japanese green tea
ice cream sandwiches

If you are eating sushi, you need to try these for dessert and have some warm sake with them.

*1 pint Green Tea ice cream
(page 78)
24 Wonton Cookies (page 123)
Thinly sliced crystallized ginger*

Remove the ice cream from the freezer to soften. Spoon enough ice cream onto a cookie so that after you put a second cookie on top and press down, the sandwich is about ½ to ¾ inch thick. Be careful when handling these cookies—they are fragile! Repeat for the remaining cookies.

Roll the sides of the cookies in thinly sliced crystallized ginger. Put them on a tray and place in the freezer for an hour or so, and then serve. *Makes 12 servings.*

○ chocolate sauce ○

This sauce is rich and mellow.

9 tablespoons unsalted butter
⅜ cup semisweet chocolate
¾ cup good quality cocoa powder
2¼ cups sugar
1 cup whipping cream
2 tablespoons liqueur, like brandy,
  Grand Marnier, or Amaretto
½ teaspoon kosher salt
1 tablespoon pure vanilla extract

To make the sauce, melt the butter with the semisweet chocolate in a saucepan over medium heat. Add the cocoa and sugar, and blend. Stir in the cream. Increase the heat a little and bring the mixture up to a boil for 10 seconds. Now add the brandy or other liqueur and simmer 1 minute.

Remove from heat and stir in the salt and vanilla. Serve warm or store in the refrigerator for up to a week. When ready to use, just warm up the amount you need and serve. *Makes 2½ cups.*

∘ hot fudge sauce ∘

This sauce is deeper, darker, lustier than the Chocolate Sauce. It was made for ice cream!

1 cup bittersweet chocolate, cut
  into small pieces
¼ cup orange blossom honey
½ cup light corn syrup
½ cup water
¾ cup good quality cocoa powder
2 teaspoons instant espresso
  coffee granules
3 tablespoons brandy or bourbon

Put the chocolate and the honey into a saucepan and melt together over low heat. Now add the remaining ingredients and blend thoroughly with a wire whip over medium heat. Bring the mixture up to a nice simmer for a few minutes, stirring constantly. The sauce is finished when it's smooth and fudge-like. *Makes 2 cups.*

° caramel sauce °

The tang of burnt sugar and cream in this sauce spell satisfaction.

1 cup sugar

2 tablespoons water

1 cup whipping cream

½ cup unsalted butter, cut
  in pieces

2 teaspoons pure vanilla extract

2 tablespoons brandy

Put the sugar and water into a saucepan and turn up the heat to high. The water should dissolve the sugar fairly quickly. The mixture will begin to cook and the idea is to burn the sugar slowly to a nice, rich deep reddish-brown, but not too dark or it will turn bitter. This may take a little practice but keep trying. The mixture is also very hot, so be careful.

Just before the sugar mixture gets to the desired color, take it off the heat and stir in the butter pieces. Slowly add the cream, being careful not to splatter.

Put the mixture back over medium heat and continue simmering for a few minutes. The sugar may ball up a little, but be patient as it will dissolve and the mixture will come together. When it does, turn up the heat a little and add the vanilla and brandy. Let it simmer 1 or 2 minutes more and remove from heat.

Serve warm or store in the refrigerator for up to a week. When ready to use, just warm up the amount you need and serve. *Makes 2 cups.*

° bachelor berries °

This is one of the simplest and best ice cream condiments you can have on hand. You can make it with either fresh or frozen berries year-round.

4 cups mixed berries (raspberries, blackberries, blueberries, strawberries)
1 cup sugar
1 cup brandy

To make, simply put the berries in a glass bowl or container. Pour the sugar and brandy over top. Stir it all up gently. The juices of the berries will blend with the sugar and brandy to form a very delicious and versatile dessert condiment. Cover tightly and store in the refrigerator for up to 2 months.

° wonton cookies °

Wonton cookies make great ice cream sandwiches. They're also good as a light and crunchy cookie on their own.

1 package (3-inch square or round)
   wonton wraps
4 tablespoons light salad oil
1 tablespoon ground cinnamon
   mixed with 1 cup granulated sugar

To make the wonton cookie, set a few paper towels to the side to drain the wontons after they have cooked. Heat the light salad oil in a 7- to 8-inch sauté pan. Heat the oil so that it is hot but not smoking. Put 1 wonton into the oil. It should take about 10 seconds for the wonton to turn a nice golden brown and become a little bubbly with air pockets. Now turn the wonton over for 10 seconds more to brown the other side.

Immediately remove the wonton to the paper towels to drain. If the wonton cooked too fast and got too dark, the oil is too hot, so turn it down a little. If it cooked too slowly, it will absorb the oil and get soggy, so turn up the heat a little. You want the wantons to be light and crispy.

Repeat this process with as many wontons as you need. As soon as each wonton has drained on the paper towels, sprinkle with some cinnamon and sugar.

condiments for
ice cream sandwiches

Finely grated chocolate

Lightly toasted sweetened flaky coconut

Thinly sliced crystallized ginger

Fresh finely ground espresso

Malted Milk powder

Milk chocolate cocoa powder

Cinnamon-sugar (5 tablespoons sugar to 1 teaspoon ground cinnamon)

Chopped toasted pecans, peanuts, or whatever nut you might want

Nutella

Warm chocolate or caramel sauce

sources

A great source of Veracruz vanilla and fabulous information on vanilla and chocolate and their history is from The Vanilla Queen at www.vanilla.com.

Some of my favorite chocolates are Callebut, Lindt, Cocoa Barry, and Ghirardelli. Many of these are carried in the chocolate section of grocery stores in small 8-ounce bars.

Most grocery stores carry crystallized ginger. It's a great condiment to keep in your pantry to use in desserts, and it's also healthy just to chew on as a natural stimulant and anti-inflammatory. Get some and you'll love it.

index

metric conversion chart

liquid and dry measures			temperature conversion chart	
U.S.	Canadian	Australian	Fahrenheit	Celsius
¼ teaspoon	1 mL	1 ml	250	120
½ teaspoon	2 mL	2 ml	275	140
1 teaspoon	5 mL	5 ml	300	150
1 tablespoon	15 mL	20 ml	325	160
¼ cup	50 mL	60 ml	350	180
⅓ cup	75 mL	80 ml	375	190
½ cup	125 mL	125 ml	400	200
⅔ cup	150 mL	170 ml	425	220
¾ cup	175 mL	190 ml	450	230
1 cup	250 mL	250 ml	475	240
1 quart	1 liter	1 litre	500	260